Selected Travel Writing

E. C. Glendenny

Other books by E. C. Glendenny

Easy Come, Easy Go

Easy on the Eyes

Easy Pickings

Resting Easy

Slow and Easy

Easy Peasy Lemon Squeezy

From Maia to Arbeia

Mudskipper Press, 2025

Paperback edition

ISBN 978 1 912226 43 6

Contents

Contents

Foreword

Hasn't travel got expensive?

I guess it is little surprise that, emerging from the ravages inflicted on both the travel and the hospitality industry by Covid, prices would rise across the sector, but the scale of the increase has been alarming. Cheap hotels are no longer cheap; expensive hotels are eye-wateringly expensive. Given the title of this book, I would like to be able to claim that this book is packed full of clever tips to save money whilst travelling, but it is sadly not the case. Like most other travellers, I have just had to suck up the additional costs and lump it. The 'Free' in 'Free and Easy' refers more to a state of mind than any kind of economic savings.

Despite this apparent prelude of woe, I still stick to the old adage that the best things in life are free, and so they are, even if it now costs an arm and a leg in order to get to some of them.

Walking has remained one of my favourite occupations during the last few years and, thankfully, as an activity it is not too taxing on the bank balance. Although it obviously costs money to travel to some walking destinations and to pay for accommodation once you arrive there, I find I can quickly forget these logistical inconveniences when I have a good walking path ahead of me, beautiful countryside surrounding me, and begin the mesmeric, left, right, left, right, of putting one sure foot in front of another, on route for a destination I often know not where.

E. C. Glendenny, January 2025

France

A Long Walk to La Défense

Although I have visited Paris on many separate occasions, I had never previously been to La Défense. After all, it is *such* a long way from the centre of town. Given this knowledge, what perverse motivation decided me to attempt to walk to it, when the Metro would have been so much easier?

My starting point was my hotel, close to the Sorbonne, on the Left Bank. I started out early, mindful of making good time along Boulevard Saint-Germain before the lunchtime crowds started to gather, cutting onto Quai des Grands Augustins somewhere slightly after Boul Mich. The Seine is a good river for walking, and I kept to my familiar Left Bank until Pont de la Concorde, where I crossed to enter the Place of the same name.

A wealthy, pony-tailed poseur was noisily and ostentatiously parking his black muscle-car outside the Hôtel de Crillon, but I was more impressed by the classic Citroën DS parked next to it.

A short stroll from here, and I am at the Grand and the Petit Palais. I make a brief loo stop and take in an exhibition—Giovanni Boldini, since you ask.

And now I am on the Champs-Élysées, with La Défense straight ahead. Some way still distant but, nevertheless, straight ahead. Don't deviate from my course, and La Défense is straight ahead. The Avenue des Champs-Élysées is crowded, but I motor past both the serious shoppers and the serious bystanders. Louis Vuitton, Dior—shame the multi-floor Citroën showroom is gone—and I am at the meeting of the ways, marked by the Arc de Triomphe. Remember, straight ahead, straight ahead, don't deviate from the route, straight ahead.

I keep straight and true along Avenue de la Grande Armée as far as Argentine, but then at Neuilly there are roadworks; major improvements; big development works, and I am forced to zig a bit, forced to zag a bit, and then, before I know it, I have made a detour, and I am heading off into the Bois de Bolougne. I justify my deviation by the fact that I have never seen the Fondation Louis Vuitton before and, while I am so close, it seems a shame not to visit it.

And then you know how it is… despite all your best intentions to keep to the straight and narrow, once you stray a bit it is just the start of a slippery slope, and you find yourself so far from your original path that there seems little point attempting to return to it. Surely there must be a quicker shortcut this way?

I cross the Seine at Pont de Puteaux passing over Île de Puteaux in the process and, before I know it, I am in the district of Puteaux itself and, unexpectedly, one of the most interesting areas of my entire walk. A surprisingly quiet enclave of quiet, cobbled streets and pretty colourful shops and cafes and houses, which look like they are from a different century to the high-rise buildings, which surround it.

But now I am lost. I know that La Défense is close but, for some reason, I cannot see it: the Grande Arche; all the skyscrapers; why are they not evident?

My transition from one world to the next is an innocuous glass elevator. A lift, which transports me from the old-world style of *vieux* Puteaux to 21st-century La Défense. It looks like the kind of lift where you are more likely to be stuck in a urine-soaked prison without recourse to help rather than a benevolent time-machine, but I put my faith in it, and my faith is duly rewarded. Five floors skywards, and here is the La Défense of my imagination, and more. I had always equated La Défense solely with the Grande Arche, but the scale of the entire area is so much more impressive.

I had known that La Défense was a major business district, but alongside the glittering glass skyscrapers is a wealth of art and sculpture and public spaces, which are genuinely innovative. The *Bright Trees* sculpture in Takis' Pool; the multi-coloured Agam Fountain; Miro's *Two Fantastic Characters*; César Baldaccini's *Thumb*. It was clearly an area, which was being used and enjoyed.

Skateboarders slalomed along the wide central boulevard; people-watchers sat on the steps of the Grande Arche; while a Korean film crew shot the latest K-Pop video against a backdrop of space-age architecture.

I rested a while on an over-sized Giant's bench—the work of artist Lilian Bourgeat—which required some considerable athletic ability even to scale, and gazed out over Le Bassin Takis where various elements of local youth jumped and splashed in the cool waters; rested, because I knew that I had the same dozen or so kilometres to wander back before I could return to my hotel once again.

A Smooth Sailing to Ushant

Ushant has something of a reputation. Ushant, also known as Ouessant, is a French island at the far southwest corner of the English Channel and the southernmost point of the Celtic Sea. It is a name, which will be familiar with sailors: Météo-France use the name Ouessant for the sea zone, which we know through the Met Office in the Shipping Forecast as Plymouth. It has a reputation for rough waters, unpredictable seas, rough crossings.

The crossing from Brest in Brittany to Ouessant takes 2 hours and 40 minutes, stopping at Le Conquet—of Asterix fame, where it is called Gesocribatum—and the island of Molène en route. The distance is 30 miles as the crow flies, and my carrier is the Penn ar Bed Compagnie Maritime. The boat is *quite* big but, not *that* big. Big enough for normal seas, but then I am reminded of that reputation for which Ushant is known.

The journey starts smoothly. There is a long leave-taking of Brest, the docks and cranes of the big port gradually disappearing, and the boat hugs the coastline to Le Conquet, passing between the narrow channel at Pointe des Espagnols on the Crozon peninsula. It is not here that I am nervous, but I know that more scary, open sea lies ahead.

In the cabin of the boat, I am amused—am I amused, or am I worried?—to notice that the container marked 'Sacs Mal de Mer' is empty. No, I am amused. I have taken my own precautions; I already have a double-layered plastic bag at the ready. I have had a previous experience of the voluminosity of vomit to know that a single plastic bag is not sufficient in extremis.

But, I am being unduly anxious. The crossing from Le Conquet to Molène could not have been smoother. I find myself not accompanied by sea-sickness but, instead, by dolphins. A small pod keep the boat company for most of its journey until landing.

And then onward to Ouessant. The outline of the island ahead is a reassuring presence. I can feel it get nearer; see it getting nearer. The sea remains blissfully calm. I cannot believe my good fortune. Nevertheless, my own fortune does not make me complacent of the potential hazards. In my imagination, I can picture the wild seas, which more frequently batter this remote island and, should I have forgotten, in the first restaurant where I stop on the island, I sit beneath a large chart titled: 'Catastrophes Maritimes abords d'Ouessant de 1860 à 1980'.

Plus, I am mindful that I still have a return journey to make.

The Lighthouses of Ushant

A consequence of the rough seas, which regularly batter the coastline around the island of Ouessant, is that it is home to a disproportionately large number of lighthouses.

There are two lighthouses located on the island itself—Phare du Stiff and Phare du Créac'h—three lighthouses offshore—Phare de la Jument, Phare de Kéréon and Phare de Nividic—not forgetting the smaller Phare de Men Korn, which is usually classified as a beacon.

Phare du Stiff is the oldest of the lighthouses, having been built by the famous French military engineer and architect Vauban in 1695. It stands close to the radar tower at Stiff Point, on one of the highest points of the island, overlooking the Iroise Sea.

Phare du Créac'h is the most powerful lighthouse in Europe, the light from which is reputedly visible from a distance of 30 miles. The building stands like a tall, straight, black-and-white stick of rock, and also houses a museum devoted to lighthouses, beacons and buoys: the Musée des Phares et Balises.

Phare de la Jument is perhaps most famous for an incident, which happened on 21 December 1989. French photographer Jean Guichard was circling the lighthouse in a helicopter during stormy weather, and captured an iconic photograph of lighthouse keeper Théodore Malgorn standing at the door of the lighthouse waiting to be rescued, as an enormous wave engulfs the entire scene all around him.

Phare de Nividic is the most westerly of the lighthouses around Ouessant and is recognisable by the spider's web construction of a helicopter pad, which sits at its summit.

Phare de Kéréon sits on Men Tensel Rock in a strait of water known as the Fromveur, which separates Ouessant from its neighbouring island, Molène.

While, Phare de Men Korn, or Tourelle de Men Korn as it is sometimes known, lies in the sea to the east of Ushant.

Perhaps even more iconic than the lighthouses themselves, are the strange structures, which stand at the edge of the sea at Pointe de Pern, in the far western corner of Ushant. It is an area of large, wave-smoothed rocks, and white frothing seas. Amidst this wild landscape, the structures rise up from the waters like ancient sea monsters; a small dragon-like head atop a long neck, reminiscent of the prow of a Viking longboat.

In reality, they are all that remain of an old cable car system, which once ran between Ouessant and the Phare de Nividic. Close to these tall pylons, a small ruined building was once the base station for the cable cars, but the entire construction was dismantled in 1945.

I sit on the rocks and gaze out over the shattered landscape, a beautifully evocative mix of nature and human construction, until a chill mist begins to roll in from the sea and I decide it is time to return to my bicycle, and make the journey back to my lodgings in Lampaul.

Instagram Street: Rue Crémieux

Instagram: it is the curse of living somewhere pretty. I count myself fortunate to live in a nondescript 2-up, 2-down of limited aesthetic appeal, such that no one would choose to stop and take a selfie in front of it. The residents of Rue Crémieux, located close to Gare de Lyon in Paris, are not so lucky. They are regularly invaded by hordes of social-media snappers, all wanting to be seen standing in front of the colourful pastel façades of their pretty row of houses.

Admittedly, some of the residents seem to go out of their way to encourage photographers, adding trompe l'œil decorations to the front of their properties, as if to stand out from their neighbours, saying 'look at me' like a Miss World contestant who claims to speak seven languages, is doing a PhD in Cosmology and who helps sick children in her spare time.

I visited Rue Crémieux very early one Sunday morning, aided by the fact that I was only staying two minutes' walk away. At that time of day, the street was deserted except for one insomniac jogger. Undoubtedly, it is a very pretty street. There are tubs with potted plants on the pavement, a cobbled carriageway, and a long double-row of tastefully colourful terraced house-fronts.

It is an oasis of Balamory in central Paris.

But Paris is a city full of beautiful streets. The Haussmann boulevards are all similarly Instagrammable. I can understand why Rue Crémieux is so popular but, in Paris, I prefer to discover beauty where it is least expected.

An Unexpected Upgrade at L'Aigle Noir

I could have made the excursion as a simple daytrip from Paris but, for some reason, I decided to make a proper job of it; give myself a bit of leisure time; be one of the first through the door; explore the forest and its environs afterwards. Anyway, this was my thinking before visiting the Château de Fontainebleau; that is why I booked in for a three-night stay at the L'Aigle Noir Hôtel.

The black eagles of the hotel's name were in plain evidence upon arrival: two sat resplendent atop the gateposts at the entrance; one, wings spread wide, resided above the clock on the hotel's roof. It was a magnificent building; if I had not known better, I could have believed that I had arrived at the Château itself. It looked as though I couldn't have chosen a better place to stay.

However, at check-in there was a hitch.

"I am very sorry, Mademoiselle, but your room is already taken."

Taken? But I had pre-booked. Pre-paid. How can this be? I attempt to adopt a suitably Gallic look of incomprehension. However, in this respect, I am hopelessly upstaged by the receptionist. My incomprehension is a mere trifle in comparison to his incomprehension; my indignation an insignificance compared to his sense of outrage. He cannot begin to understand how such a travesty could have occurred.

Thankfully, he has a solution.

"We do have *one* other room available, Mademoiselle."

I put on a show of moderate resistance before acquiescing, as we both know that I will.

"Very well," I say, rather ill-spiritedly, "but don't think I'm paying extra for breakfast," I assert, pointing at the price: €22. Outrageous!

Still grumbling to myself, I allow a porter to take my bags and direct me to my new room. I am still feeling mildly-aggrieved by the mix-up; imagine myself being allotted the pokiest, most undesirable room in the entire establishment. I follow closely in the porter's footsteps, giving my best pretence of being in a huff. He unlocks a door and we begin to walk along a long corridor. My huff increases. How much further must we go? When will we ever get to *my* room? We go up a short flight of carpeted stairs; pass a room to the right with an open door. There are display cabinets on the left side of the corridor. And still we walk on. Another open door on the right. It looks a bit like a bathroom. For Goodness sake, where is this room of mine? Tucked away in the most remote dead-end? My huff was beginning to reach fever pitch. Until it suddenly dawned on me. This *was* my room. We had actually entered my room at the locked door. This was *all* my room. The long corridor, the staircase, the rooms to the right, the display cabinets to the left, the bathroom—with briefly-spotted Jacuzzi bath—and now the enormous room at the end of the corridor, with a bed, which would have comfortably accommodated the entire Les Bleus, plus reserves.

My huff evaporates as quickly as it had appeared. The result of my modestly-priced original room having been double-booked was a free upgrade to the best suite in the hotel. Marie Antoinette herself could not have been more chuffed.

Even so, I still didn't have breakfast. €22. I'm not made of money. I bought a €2 croissant each morning in the town, and then took great pleasure taking it back to my room and eating it on my queen-sized bed.

Germany

Oberammergau: Five Top Tips

After a two-year Covid delay, the 42nd Oberammergau Passion Play runs until 2 October 2022.

Five days a week (Tue, Thu, Fri, Sat and Sun) during the summer, the Passion Play Theatre will host somewhere in the region of 5,000 spectators each day, travelling from all around the world, and a similar number of local villagers taking either on-stage acting, or off-stage supporting roles, not to mention the odd goat, horse and camel, too.

Here are my five top tips to best enjoy the performance.

Let the Train Take the Strain

Although there are two large Park & Ride car parks on the outskirts of Oberammergau village and shuttle buses to the event site, I found travelling by train the most relaxing way to arrive at Oberammergau.

Only a couple of hours from Munich Hbf, with a change of trains in Murnau, and passing through beautiful Bavarian countryside of lakes and mountains, the train was surprisingly empty, and the station at Oberammergau a peaceful haven in which to arrive and get your bearings.

Photography in the Performance is not Permitted

The instructions, which accompany your Oberammergau ticket are quite ferocious. There is a long list of dos and don'ts, which make it sound as though it may take hours of queuing simply to enter the Passion Play site. In practice, I found the admissions process swift, smooth, and friendly.

However, one thing that is clamped down upon is any photography of the actual performance. It was possible to take photographs of the stage prior to the performance, but while the play was underway, anyone attempting to take photographs or video were politely—but firmly—requested to stop.

Brush Up Your Local Accent

The entire Passion Play is in German and, not just German, but Austro-Bavarian German. My companion was a fluent German speaker, but she struggled to understand quite a lot of the thick, local dialect.

I, on the other hand, who can't understand a single word of the language, still found the entire performance enthralling.

Pre-book an Interval Meal

The Passion Play runs for five hours. Five hours! That is a bum-numbingly long time to be sitting still. Thankfully, this period is split up into two sessions of two and a half hours each, with an interval of three hours.

During this break, it is likely that you are going to want to get a meal for yourself and, although Oberammergau has a plethora of eating-places, most of these will have been pre-booked months in advance. I was fortunate enough that the Youth Hostel, where I was staying, took pity on me, and managed to conjure up something to eat for me during the interval, otherwise it would have been a choice between take-away pizza or whatever I could find to eat on the hoof from Edeka.

Spend Some Extra Days to Explore the Countryside

Oberammergau is located on the edge of the Ammergau Alps in Bavaria, close to Germany's border with Austria's Tyrol. It is a beautiful countryside of mountains and forests and rivers, and a lovely location for hiking. There are several easy walks alongside the river Ammer directly out of Oberammergau, and plenty more serious hikes to some of the nearby summits.

For a daytrip, the fairytale castle of Neuschwanstein is only 25 kilometres away as the crow flies.

For those planning to visit Oberammergau to see the Passion Play, it is definitely worth extending your trip to spend some time exploring the rest of the region.

Oberammergau and Unterammergau

Oberammergau and Unterammergau is the tale of two villages.

The two villages lie about three miles distant from one another, both on the banks of the Ammer River, in the district of Garmisch-Partenkirchen in the Bavarian Alps.

What differentiates the villages is an event that happened almost four hundred years ago.

At the time, Europe was being ravished by bubonic plague, and the disease had even reached the remote southwestern corner of Germany in which lie Oberammergau and Unterammergau. The residents of Oberammergau made a vow to God that if their village was spared the plague, they would all perform a Passion Play every ten years to give thanks for their survival. According to legend, after the vow was made not another villager died from the plague, and the first Passion Play in Oberammergau was performed in 1634. The tradition has been carried on faithfully every ten years since, with the 42nd Passion Play taking place in 2022.

There is no doubt that the advent of the Passion Play transformed the village of Oberammergau. Today, the village is geared up to receive a daily influx of 5,000 tourists from all over the world; there are restaurants and lodgings; car parks and gift shops; and the daily ticket receipts for the Passion Play itself must total something in the region of half a million Euros.

In contrast, just a short distance along the valley, Unterammergau looks largely unchanged from how I can imagine it must have looked back in the early 17th century. It has a sleepy, timeless feel of tranquillity. The focus of the village remains the 11th century chapel of St Leonhard. There are horses in the fields; hay piled in the barns; chopped wood in the sheds. There are few visitors and, the locals who I met, still wear traditional lederhosen and dirndls, without either a sense of inhibition or irony.

I wonder which village envies the other more? Does Unterammergau feel jealous of the commercial behemoth next door, or does Oberammergau rue the innocence that they have lost?

E. C. Glendenny tries to get her head around the local tongue-twister:

Heut kommt der Hans zu mir,
Freut sich die Lies.
Ob er aber über Oberammergau,
Oder aber über Unterammergau,
Oder aber überhaupt nicht kommt,
Ist nicht gewiss.

A Daytrip to the Kehlsteinhaus

I say a daytrip, but that requires some qualification. A daytrip has to start and end somewhere. You would be hard-pushed to make this a daytrip from New York, for example. Or from London. Or even from Munich. And believe me, I did look into it. My daytrip starts and ends in Salzburg, which might seem somewhat surprising given that the Eagle's Nest (or the Kehlsteinhaus) lies in Germany and Salzburg is in Austria but, as far as major stopping-off points are concerned, Salzburg is closer to the Kehlsteinhaus than any other city.

I take an organised tour. Once again, I had looked into alternatives, but gave them all up as hopelessly impractical without my own transport. So, I find myself on an early morning Panoramatours' coach, setting off from Mirabell Square, in the company of fifty strangers, journeying the relatively modest distance of twenty-five kilometres south to our first rendezvous point, the slightly ominously named Documentation Centre.

Despite its intimidatingly officious name, the Documentation Centre proves to be little more than a big carpark. But it is here that a

change of transport is required. The Salzburg coach is abandoned; a new bus and new driver, one experienced on the winding, mountain roads, which lead up the Kehlstein, takes command.

The scenery of the Berchtesgaden Alps is stunning. The higher the bus climbs, increasingly more expansive the view. Until eventually… another carpark.

Here, though, there is a mysterious brick-vaulted tunnel leading into the mountainside. It is wide enough to take a Mercedes 'Grosser' but, instead, we walk. At the end of the tunnel is a lift. For such a rural location, it is a surprisingly ornate lift, decorated in gleaming brass and brightly reflecting mirrors. And, at the summit of the lift? Well, nowadays, a rather boring café.

It is a long way to come for such an anti-climax. Of course, the reality is that few people travel all the way to the Kehlsteinhaus simply to sample the current *plat du jour.* The tunnel, lift and mountain-top building were all originally designed by Martin Bormann to provide a meeting-place for senior Nazi Party members during World War Two. It was a favourite location for Adolf Hitler. And it is not hard to see why. The location of the Kehlsteinhaus is spectacular. It is easy to see why it is known as the Eagle's Nest.

There are panoramic views in all directions of the surrounding mountains, and of the town of Berchtesgaden to the northwest. Very little sign of the building's inglorious history still exists.

At the time of my visit—early on in the season in May; the roads being impassable for much of the winter—there was still deep snow laying on the mountainside, making any ventures off the designated path a foolish endeavour. The sun is shining bright and, despite the altitude, it is not cold. The Kehlsteinhaus becomes secondary to the majesty of its surroundings. It is a day to be outside in optimistic nature; not tracing the history of a dark past.

However, my organised tour is operating to a tight schedule, and there is only so much time permitted to stand and stare. Soon, the bus is backtracking down the mountainside, for a lunch stop at the picturesque town of Berchtesgaden.

Overshadowed, in many ways, by its close proximity to the Eagle's Nest, Berchtesgaden is a pleasant place to while away a few hours. Unlike my fellow travellers, most of whom descend upon the comfy chairs and hearty dishes of the nearest restaurant, I grab a sandwich that I can eat on the hoof, and attempt to walk as many of the streets of the small, alpine town as I can manage before my coach's allotted departure time.

Once past the initial barrage of glitzy souvenir shops selling various items of lederhosen and local delicacies, I soon find myself in Schlossplatz facing the impressive frontages of Stiftskirche St Peter und Johannes der Täufer, the Königliches Schloss Berchtesgaden, and the cloisters with their murals depicting Berchtesgaden's history.

I am torn between stopping to investigate each building or exploring further afield; all the time, I am conscious of the ticking clock of organised tourism; can almost hear the driver of the Panoramatours' coach beginning to rev his engine, anxious to be back in Salzburg ahead of schedule.

In the end, it is the beauty of the mountains, which calms me; halts me. On all sides, it is the snowy peaks, which dominate the view. It is their natural history, which should be celebrated in this beautiful corner of Germany. I find a quiet bench, take out my sandwich, and end up simply sitting and enjoying the view.

Dinner at Yenidze

A former cigarette factory does not seem the most obvious place to have an evening meal, but Yenidze in Dresden is not your average cigarette factory.

Looking like a multi-storey mosque in the Moorish Revival style, the Yenidze Tobacco and Cigarette Factory was first opened in 1909. The building has a huge, decorated dome and ornate chimneys designed to look like minarets. Falling into long disuse after the Second World War, the building is now an office block and restaurant.

However, skirting the exotic exterior, the restaurant is not easy to locate. The grand main entrance to the building is shut up, and the only way in appears to be a rather unprepossessing gateway, leading to a short flight of steps and a small backdoor. A small sign displays a menu card, otherwise I might not have had the nerve to venture further, but whether the sign is still valid or a relic of a decade past, it is not easy to tell.

Slightly daunted, I go in. The doorway reveals a short, undecorated corridor, ending at a small lift. If in doubt, go to the top. I press the button for the top floor and, rather to my surprise, the lift whirrs into action.

When the lift stops, I am pleasantly surprised to find myself in what appears to be a restaurant; tables and chairs; tablecloths and cutlery. However, there is not a single diner in sight, nor any staff on duty. I am still not sure that I haven't stumbled upon something that closed years beforehand.

I call out tentatively, which has the effect of producing a middle-aged woman from a back room:

"What do you want?"

"Are you open?" I ask nervously.

"We're full," is the rather unexpected reply.

My gaze across the empty tables must have voiced my doubt of this claim, because it is followed up with:

"Try downstairs."

I am shown to a small staircase leading to the floor below. Little did I realise it, but that short staircase was like a wardrobe to Narnia.

Here, there was not only a restaurant, but a busy, open-air, rooftop restaurant, with glorious panoramic views across the entire Dresden skyline. Here, there were customers and uniformed waitresses; plates of food and tankards of beer. I was guided to a table, with a view looking out towards the Elbe. It was beyond my expectations as a place to eat.

I was conventional in my choice of food: schnitzel, washed down with a big pint of beer. The early evening atmosphere was very peaceful. Above me the huge dome and tapering minarets of the building were within touching distance; below, the streets and houses of Dresden a different world. It felt like I was floating on a magic carpet, alone amongst the clouds in a *One Thousand and One Nights* fantasy.

I finished my food, and watched the sun begin to descend beyond the horizon. By the time I reached my hotel, it had begun to rain. Return to reality.

Cologne Cathedral: No Lift, No Joke

It was only meant to be an overnight stop; a brief break in my journey between the Eurostar in Brussels and travelling on to Berlin, 350 miles further east. It is amazing just how much it is possible to cram into a few short hours in a city, though.

Cologne. You can't visit Cologne and not see the cathedral. Well, can you? Quite literally, there it is, bang, right outside as soon as I stepped off the train.

I could quote all the stats—tallest twin-spired church in the world; the largest façade of any church in the world—but the simple fact is that it dominates the city.

As I have written before, I am someone who can rarely resist the lure of a tall tower and, despite my time being limited, I knew that I wouldn't rest until I had experienced the view from the summit.

The entrance to the tower of Cologne Cathedral—it is the southern one, which is accessible—is outside the main cathedral, around the side of the building, and *down* some steps to a modern vestibule.

Ignoring the small exhibition and gift shop, and conscious that my seconds in the city were rapidly slipping away, I paid my €6 entrance fee, and set off up the tower like a ferret up a Yorkshireman's trouser leg. In my haste, I was only vaguely conscious of two signs, which I was invited to read before I set off. One said: *Kein Aufzug, Kein Scherz*; No Lift, No Joke. Against the instruction, I did find this notice funny. The other sign stated precisely how many steps had to be climbed in order to reach the tower-top. I barely paused to take in the words of this sign; only allowing the information it conveyed to enter my conscious mind when I was already several spirals into my ascent and, by then, I couldn't recall what the sign had actually said. 133 steps, was it? I wasn't sure. It didn't seem like very many. I felt as though I must be almost halfway there already. I was pretty sure I had climbed more than that in the Campanile in Florence or when going up the Leaning Tower of Pisa. I'd be up and down in a jiffy, with plenty of time to spare before my onward journey.

But the stone spiral staircase went on and on. I felt sure I must have already climbed more than 133 steps. Finally, an end of sorts came into sight. It was heralded by a deafening peal of bells, and I found myself emerging onto an internal, wooden bell-platform, where a solitary official sat in a small booth. I hoped for the sake of this Quasimodo security guard's hearing that it was sound-proofed.

But that was not the top of the tower. Nowhere near it. The stone spiral staircase continued. I lost count of the number of steps. I came to a second platform. This one was exposed to the elements––on this particular day a fine rain, which made the metal platform quite slippery. Flights of metal stairs ascended onwards and, where they went, I followed. Finally, I came to a narrow, spiral metal staircase. Not a minute too soon. The muscles of my legs were beginning to demand an explanation. They had received no adequate forewarning of the exertion, which would be expected of them. Surely the summit was now in sight?

And there it was. An external stone walkway traversing the circumference of the southern tower at a height of about 97 metres above ground level. Through the intricate Gothic tracery, the views across Cologne and down to the Rhine below were wonderful, and this despite the mist, which was trying its best to envelope the scene.

Here, too, was another security guard, also isolated in his own private booth. So isolated that I was unable to ask him all the questions which immediately sprung to my mind: does he like heights; does he go back down to ground level for his lunchbreak; is there not somewhere a secret, private lift?

From this lofty proximity, it was apparent that some of the ornamental masonry of the tower has been broken and lost, and some of the twiddly bits—is that the proper architectural term?—had fallen in the past. In some places, netting had been secured to prevent any further collapses. Similarly, a perilous-looking iron ladder, which leads up to the very peak of the tower, another 60 metres higher, was blocked off to even the most intrepid public.

My legs were already feeling weak from the ascent, and I was only too conscious of an equivalent descent still to make. It was a rather more slow-moving, wobbly and dizzy person who finally stopped to properly read the notice at the bottom of the tower some little time later.

533 steps. Not 133.

Would I have started out, if I had known this beforehand?

Of course I would. Now, just point me in the direction of Ulm Cathedral, and the tallest single church spire in Europe.

Riding the Reichstag Whirlwind

It isn't every day that an email turns up addressed to me from the Deutscher Bundestag, complete with its official federal-eagle crest.

The substance of the email was to give me permission to visit the roof terrace and dome of the Reichstag Building in Berlin.

It was fortunate that I had checked the website for visitors to the Reichstag prior to arrival; several days' notice is required to gain admittance; it is not somewhere you can just turn up willy-nilly, on spec.

I have always admired the design of the Reichstag's dome. Designed by Norman Foster and built by Waagner-Biro, the construction is meant to symbolise the reunification of Germany post-1989. For me, though, rather than invoking something that brings people together, I have always thought that the central column of the Reichstag's dome is reminiscent of a rapidly-rotating whirlwind, tearing everything asunder.

It is a beautiful construction: the glass dome, more simply symmetrical than the similar 'glass bollock' of London's City Hall; the interwoven, twin spiral ramps, reminiscent of Bramante's staircase in the Vatican Museums or Frank Lloyd Wright's at the Guggenheim; and the mirrored cone at its core.

The mirrors on this glass vortex are positioned such that it is possible to view the democratic workings of the Bundestag in the chamber below the dome; in practice, most visitors use them simply to find a reflection of themselves in order to take a selfie. Or is that just me?

Climbing the ramp to the summit of the dome affords wonderful 360° views across the Berlin skyline; from the darkly-wooded green expanse of the Tiergarten to the west; to the olive-spiked cocktail stick of the Berliner Fernsehturm and Alexanderplatz to the east.

Reaching the top of the dome, there is a circular, wooden bench, upon which, sprawling full-length, it is possible to lie flat, looking directly up at the sky above. I hog a prone position contemplating the great beyond for longer than is my due but, I am not just idly cloud-gazing, I am conscientiously watching out for whirlwinds.

Staying at the Bauhaus

This was a genuine thrill. I had booked to stay a night at the Bauhaus in Dessau, not quite knowing what to expect. The cost of the room for one night was very reasonable, although the picture on the website indicated that it might be somewhat… spartan. But, that was just what I wanted. For me, the essence of the Bauhaus was minimalism; I wanted clear straight lines, simple geometric forms; no sentimentality.

The instructions I received with my booking informed me that I could collect my room key from an administration room in the main Bauhaus complex. Here I was met by a kindly gentleman who, along with my key, gave me directions to both my room and the breakfast café. He also took great pains to stress to be careful if I stood on the balcony. Balcony? My heart leapt. It couldn't be…?

I began to follow the directions to my room, thought I could take a short cut, discovered I couldn't, found myself hopelessly lost. Thankfully, the kindly gentleman was leaning out of his window, anticipating this event. With a friendly wave and a pointed finger, he soon had me back on the right track.

The guestrooms for the Bauhaus are in the original student block, dating from the mid-1920s. My room was on the third floor, up a bare concrete staircase, devoid of ornamentation. Along a corridor, past the toilet and showers, the last door on the left. On the left. It was all-important.

I opened the door to my room, and I couldn't have been more delighted. The room was actually much larger than I had anticipated; as former student room go, it was positively palatial. It was decorated simply, but perfectly comfortably, and had a large window, with a beautiful view looking out towards Dessau itself. And it had a balcony. Rooms on the left side of the corridor have a balcony; those on the right do not.

And why this obsession with the balcony? Because it was a black and white photograph of the iconic Bauhaus balconies by László Moholy-Nagy, which got me fascinated by the Bauhaus and the School of Art, Design and Architecture, which is based there, in the first place.

But, I could see why the kindly gentleman had warned me to be careful about the balcony. Despite the fact that the Bauhaus has been restored and renovated, some aspects of the classic modernist design would not necessarily pass current-day stringent health and safety checks. The balconies were devastatingly beautiful to look at; slightly perilous to stand on with their low hand-rails.

I spent my entire time at the Bauhaus in a state of blissful enthrallment. Every smallest detail from door handle to sink plug to floor tile appeared iconic to me.

Outside the building, it was amusing to watch the modern generation of students who currently study there nonchalantly chatting, locking up their bicycles, rushing to grab a bite to eat in the café. Doing all the humdrum things that students at any college or university around the world do. For them, the building was ordinary, just part of their everyday world of study and life. Just how it should be; just what the Bauhaus stands for: uncomplicated; functional; utilitarian.

E. C. Glendenny cannot recommend staying a night (or two) at the Bauhaus highly enough.

Lundy

Lundy: 25 Years of Change and Constancy

On the way to Lundy, I stopped off for lunch with an old friend who lives in the mid-Devon countryside, and whom I hadn't seen for many years. At first, I found myself focusing on the differences I noticed in my friend since the last time I had seen her but, very quickly, we slipped into an old familiarity, and all I then saw were the similarities. And it was much the same story visiting Lundy.

It had been 25 years since I had last been on Lundy. It was a fact that I was quick to impart to the warden attending the reception room on the island: "I doubt you'll find much has changed," she replied.

Oh, but it had. At first, all I could spot about the island were the differences from when I had last been there, the largest being the landing bay where I first came ashore. 25 years earlier, no form of landing stage for the boat from the mainland had existed. Back then, the MS Oldenburg was required to anchor several hundred yards offshore in the lee of the island, and visitors and luggage were transported from the boat to dry(ish) land—there was usually a bit of inevitable foot-wetting—by tender. Now a wooden jetty links with a concrete incline which, in turn, joins to a navigable pathway winding up the cliff side to the village.

There were changes in the village, too. A long construction of low wooden dwellings, perhaps to house some of the island's temporary workers; and an expansion of the Marisco Tavern into the Wheelhouse, which permits space for a long, additional bar-counter, from which to order food. The menu at the Marisco Tavern has expanded, too. Previously, the choice had been fairly limited, centred around lamb, and whatever fish had been caught fresh that day—I remember a big skate one day; now, there are vegetarian options; a ubiquitous game pie—to be recommended—and even a range of desserts.

The farm appeared larger, too, with a wider range of livestock; I didn't recall seeing Highland Cattle on my previous visit, but several of the big beasts now roamed shaggily along the main path, south of Halfway Wall.

Even the Old Light had not remained unchanged. Although its spiral stone staircase remained memorably vertiginous, the deckchairs at its summit have been updated from ones with a red striped canvas to ones with a green striped canvas—I'm getting pernickety now, I realise—and it is no longer possible to access the perilous exterior parapet which, given the state of the rusty metal of the balustrade is probably just as well.

One thing that was unaltered, though. The beautiful natural view from the top of the Old Light across the entire island, both north and south. Timeless.

No Such Thing as Bad Weather

It was Alfred Wainwright who wrote that 'There is no such thing as bad weather, only unsuitable clothing'. I am not sure that seasoned fell-walker had ever stayed on Lundy during a run of Atlantic storms when he made the observation, but I am prepared to concede there is something in the wisdom. Particularly since I happen to be a woman who is the proud possessor of a pair of waterproof over-trousers.

I know that I have sung the praises of these trousers before, during my walk along Hadrian's Wall, but I think another eulogy is due. I cannot recommend them highly enough; even in the dampest conditions—and Lundy in July 2023 was damp—nothing gets past these trousers!

Since my Hadrian's Wall walk, I have also added to my rambling kit a waterproof cover for my rucksack—surely an improvement on the plastic carrier bag, which I had fashioned to serve the purpose in the past? Sadly, this has proved less of a success; where the plastic cover doesn't fit perfectly, rain still manages to find its way through to the bag beneath. Admittedly, it is more waterproof than my previous Heath Robinson construction although, strangely, not so satisfying.

The View from the 'Blue Bung'

I never bore of watching the sea. From the top of the stone front steps of the Old School—or 'Blue Bung' as it is affectionately known—on Lundy, I have a wide vista of water outstretched before me; the coasts of Wales and North Devon low smudges on a distant horizon.

In the lee of the island, the Bristol Channel lies pacifically unruffled by even the smallest ripple; today, an iron-clad grey beneath thick white clouds above.

Of course, it is not the sea alone that I am watching. Privately, I hope that any moment that serene surface will suddenly be shattered by a free-leaping harbour porpoise, or pierced by the black fin of a cruising basking shark.

And, here, the wind and waters conspire to deceive me; endlessly combining to create a wave, which looks like a lurking leviathan, or a patch of ripples, which appear as a dark sub-aquatic object swimming away from the shore.

But, I am also aware, that whilst scanning for signs of marine life, my perception of scale is hopelessly adrift. In a view that spans for several miles in width, and many more in depth, I am anticipating my leaping porpoise or gliding shark's fin to occupy a significant prominence; expect it to stand out large and clear in visual proportion to the size of the keenness of my observation.

The reality is that if ever I am fortunate enough that either a porpoise or shark should rise within my field of vision, it would be a tiny speck measured against the vastness of the surroundings. I must refocus my eyes to look closer; train my brain to think smaller.

I make a conscious effort to observe the water nearer to the shore where I stand more chance of making a sighting, but my imagination continually draws my eyes back towards the horizon, ever hopeful of spotting sea monsters.

The Siren Call of Lundy

At first, it was hard to distinguish the sound from that of the wind. But, when I listened more closely, it had a different note to it; something hollower and altogether more melancholic.

I wondered if it was perhaps a baby crying, but from where? There was no one around. For miles. But surely it was a cry of some kind? It was a mournful sound; redolent with despair; surely a plea for help?

I was reminded of the legend of the Sirens; those creatures from Greek mythology whose seductive cries almost lured Odysseus and his crew to a watery grave. This sound had a similarly alluring quality, compelling investigation. The Siren call of Lundy.

It was not until I spotted a grey shape in the sea far below me that I realised the origin of the strange noise. Seals. Atlantic Grey Seals to be precise. Cutting into the peace of the island, the sound of their wails was echoing up to me standing on the cliffs above.

Passing on from the bay where I had spotted the seals, I met a fellow cliff-top walker, having a picnic lunch above Brazen Ward. I told her about the strange sounds I had heard.

"Maybe you've something of the Selkie in you," she suggested. "If you can hear the seals talking."

I thought this was perhaps a rather fanciful notion. I hadn't been staying on Lundy for long enough to be so swept up in island folklore. However, although I didn't admit it to my fellow-traveller, I could have sworn that one of the seals had waved at me.

Austria

Stephansdom: South or North Tower?

There are many things to marvel about in St Stephen's Cathedral, Vienna: the crypts; the bells; the catacombs; its gothic pulpit; the chapels; the décor; not forgetting its iconic roof, made up of almost a quarter of a million multi-coloured glazed tiles.

However, for me, as Cologne or even Rye can bear witness, I find it hard to be reverential when there is an opportunity to gain a high vantage point.

At St Stephen's Cathedral, there is a choice of two towers to scale: the south and the north ones. The Südturm—affectionately known as Steffl—and the Nordturm. The south tower requires climbing up 343 stairs to its summit. The north tower, by contrast, is shorter and accessible by a lift. Strictly for wimps. It is the south tower for me.

The 343 steps appeared rather a modest challenge after Cologne's 533, but St Stephen's had a few surprises up its sleeve. The first of which was where to find the entrance. It was tucked away outside the cathedral, hidden behind a parked van at the time that I visited.

The first 200+ steps of the ascent are up a very narrow stone spiral staircase unrelieved by any form of landing or stopping-off point. It is one long continuous dizzying climb.

Relief eventually appears in the shape of an even narrower stone corridor and a tiny—strictly one-person—ancient wooden seat, of which I duly make service. After that, the final climb to the summit is child's play.

Tantalisingly, the staircase continues further, but it is blocked off to the public, such that almost half of Steffl's height is out of bounds. Instead, I am directed through a wooden door to the Watch Room, an internal gallery about 67 metres above street level, with 360° views from its windows across the city. It is not quite the thrill of emerging onto an open-air gantry—which is the case from the North Tower––but still well worth the climb.

Following Harry Lime Down the Vienna Sewers

A flimsy hairnet combined with a white plastic helmet is not necessarily my best look, but they were compulsory kit to undertake the Dritte Mann hour-long tour of the Vienna sewers.

The sewers were made famous when they appeared in the famous chase sequence in Carol Reed's 1949 film *The Third Man*, starring Orson Welles as black marketeer Harry Lime. Ironically, Welles only spent a small amount of time in the genuine sewers; many of his scenes being shot in a studio in London and, rather than squeeze through one of the more traditional narrow sewer entrances, Welles is seen entering by what is now known as the 'Hollywood Entrance', which was wider and had easy steps spiralling downwards. I'm not knocking him, though; that was the same way by which I entered the sewers, in a corner of Karlsplatz.

The tour was led by a genuine Viennese sewer-worker, who interspersed an interesting commentary with a series of wisecracks mainly to do with the black humour of sewer work.

Lights on our helmets illuminated the way down into the sewer's depths but, on an occasion when we were asked to turn our lights off, an impenetrable darkness prevailed. Into this darkness was projected a series of stills from *The Third Man* movie, including the iconic image of Harry Lime himself.

We pass through narrow tunnels, the sound of rushing sewer-water never far away. I had been warned about the smell of the sewers, but there was nothing that was too unpleasant; perhaps it was just that after a busy day of sightseeing in Vienna, I smelled just as bad as the sewers, so couldn't tell the difference?

Eventually the tunnels opened out into a vast, subterranean, domed cavern. Here the River Wien runs underground through the capital, emerging into the open air again at a point in Stadtpark, a kilometre or so to the northeast. At times of heavy rain, much of the cavern becomes impassable.

Although I had always enjoyed the film *The Third Man*, what I actually found most interesting about the Dritte Mann tour was seeing the conditions, and hearing about the experiences, of real sewer workers in the city. For me, being in the tunnels was atmospheric and exciting; for a sewer-worker the same environment represents hard graft, cramped conditions and a day-to-day normality, but our guide spoke with a real sense of pride and job-satisfaction about how he and his colleagues kept this vital utility beneath Vienna operating smoothly.

Not a Gist on the Wiener Riesenrad

It was a fairly natural extension of my *The Third Man* themed day in Vienna that I should want to take a spin on the Riesenrad. I'd been down the sewers; now it was time to be transported into the skies.

Besides, I had always wanted to take a ride on Vienna's famous big Ferris wheel. I don't know why I had never done this before when I had visited Vienna in the past?

I suppose part of the reason might have been because it is located out in Prater, 3.5kms northeast of the city centre; an easy-enough train ride from Karlsplatz, but not somewhere that I would have considered readily walkable.

This time, though, I did make the effort to get out to Prater. And I wasn't the only one. When I got there, it was packed. It appeared that half of Vienna and their families had decided to spend that afternoon at the amusement park. There was an hour-long queue for the Riesenrad.

However, 'Patience' is not my middle-name for nothing – *clearly, given your initials, 'Patience' is not your middle-name at all; although 'Composure' might substitute. (Ed.)*

I waited as the queue lined up to pay; as the queue snaked around an exhibition of Riesenrad memorabilia; as the queue reached the open-air. When did this become a thing with queues: the queue within a queue? Just when you think you have reached the end of one queue, you realise that it is only the start of the next queue. Nevertheless, by the time I had reached the al fresco element of the queue, at least the big wheel was in sight, looming large above me.

I took considerable pleasure watching the antics surrounding every fourth compartment of the big wheel; these had been converted into private dining cars. Each time one of these cars drew level to the embarkation platform, a uniformed waiter would emerge as if by magic, hurry into the carriage, and replace one course of the guests' dining experience for the next one. I speculated about whether slow-eaters would have time to complete their meal between each rotation?

But then, suddenly, there I was. Front of the queue, and being ushered into a carriage, along with a dozen or so fellow travellers. And before I knew it, we were off and up.

Amidst admiring the views of Vienna – even spotting distant Schloss Schönbrunn, where I had visited three days earlier – I rather forgot about my intentions of following in Harry Lime's footsteps. The bright daylight of a late-summer afternoon might have had something to do with it. My memories of *The Third Man* are of a city cloaked in perpetual twilight; atop the Riesenrad, the over-riding impression was one of supreme clarity.

But, how wrong could I be. Clarity was the very last thing that I had in my possession at that moment.

It was not until I reached home, several weeks later, that I gained any kind of real insight. Feeling nostalgic regarding my previous visit to Vienna, I went in search of the photographs I had taken at that time. And there they were, at the end of a pack of rather blurry snaps, two pictures taken at the Prater from close on thirty years' prior: the Riesenrad from ground level and, more telling, a view of Vienna, clearly taken from the summit of the giant Ferris wheel.

I'd been there before; been to Prater; ridden the wheel; done it all before; practically taken identical photographs. Did I remember any of it? Not a jot. Not even a false memory; just plain forgotten.

Within the field of False Memory research, Valerie Reyna and Charles Brainerd talking about Fuzzy-trace theory, suggest that humans store information in two distinct ways: verbatim and gist. Verbatim is clear and precise; gist is fuzzy and indistinct.

While I like to believe that I walk through much of life in something of a continuous state of fuzzy-trace, when it comes to the Riesenrad, I don't even have a gist.

Sachertorte or Strudel at Café Bel Étage?

Never let it be said that I am someone who avoids a travel cliché. Vienna and chocolate cake go practically hand-in-hand. It would almost be a crime to visit Vienna and not have a slice. The only question is, which café to visit?

Synonymous with Sachertorte is Café Sacher at the Sacher Hotel in Philharmoniker Strasse. I arrived on a wet and overcast day, and the queue for afternoon tea in the main café was stretching outside along the pavement, hopeful diners forming a bedraggled, umbrella-holding line. However, just around the corner, a cut-out pavement sign of a young man dressed in a smart uniform and natty hat, and holding a tray on which was displayed the fabled Sachertorte, directed my steps towards an inside counter, from where I was instructed to take the stairs to the first floor, to be immediately seated in the luxurious surroundings of the Café Bel Étage.

Seats of sumptuous maroon upholstery with thickly padded backs lined the large room. Three window booths held a particular appeal, overlooking the busy thoroughfare below. For the sake of form, I looked at the menu, although I already knew what I intended to order. But then again…

Isn't apple strudel almost as much a Vienna cliché as is Sachertorte? Suddenly, I was in a dilemma. Sachertorte or strudel? They both looked very good. What to choose?

In the end, it was no dilemma at all. When in doubt, have both.

And, if I was called upon to choose a favourite out of the two? To my surprise, I would actually plump for the strudel. Now, don't get me wrong: the Sachertorte was very nice, no complaints whatsoever on that score, it was just that the strudel was genuinely divine; light and sweet and tasty.

Returning outside, so full of sugar that I no longer noticed the drizzle, my thoughts began to turn to where I might go for dinner.

UK

YHA Exclusive Hire: A Contradiction in Terms?

Something odd is happening at the YHA. I am sure that it is a pragmatic thing. But, I am not sure that it is a good thing.

The Youth Hostels Association's stated aim is: "To help all, especially young people of limited means, to a greater knowledge, love and care of the countryside, and appreciation of the cultural values of towns and cities, particularly by providing youth hostels or other accommodation for them in their travels, and thus to promote their health, recreation and education."

That statement pretty much sums up the YHA as I know it. I have been a grateful guest at several of their hostels in a number of different locations around Britain and, via Hostelling International, a network of hostels spread around the world, most recently staying in the DJH Jugendherberge in Oberammergau. You know what you are going to get: simple accommodation; basic facilities; good value; often wonderful locations.

Since its inception in 1930, the YHA has been a lifeline for countless travellers; walkers; holiday-makers, wanting to gain access to some remote corners of Britain's beautiful countryside, not to mention affordable stays in some of our towns and cities.

So, what is YHA Exclusive Hire?

Now, I'll admit, my current crusade is provoked by something of a personal grievance, rather than some deep-rooted commitment to egalitarianism. The fact is, I fancied walking the Pembrokeshire Coastal Path. Maybe not all of it. But the northern section. From St Dogmael's around to Martin's Haven. It would have been close on 100 miles. A decent-enough challenge. So, I started to make preparations.

I split my route up into eight sections, planning to walk roughly twelve miles a day. I began to hunt out suitable accommodation where I could stay each night. There was a nice-looking B&B overlooking the beach at Broad Haven; a fancy inn for a bit of R&R at Porthgain; a possible glamping pod, I'd got my eye on, south of Solva. However, on some sections of the route, the choice of accommodation was severely limited; this was relatively wild, remote territory, far removed from any villages or basic amenities. Thank God, then, for the YHA.

The hostel at Pwll Deri looked as though it was going to provide a lifeline; somewhere that I could rest my weary head on the long, off-the-beaten-track section between Fishguard and Porthgain. On top of that, the location of the hostel looked absolutely stunning. The reviews by previous walkers who had stayed there had all been absolutely glowing: "breathtaking views"; "awesome location"; "great value for money". I tried to make an online booking for a bed for one night. And that was how I first encountered YHA Exclusive Hire.

It was no longer possible to book a bed for one night. Not even possible to book a private room. You had to book the entire hostel, for a minimum stay of two nights, at a cost of £399 per night. That meant shelling out the best part of eight hundred quid for a simple bed. And this was one of the cheaper periods. Other dates were priced at £599 per night; some more at £749 per night. Admittedly, I'd get the choice of 28 different beds spread across seven separate rooms all to myself, but it was not really what I was looking for. What had happened to the ethos of helping "young people of limited means"? This seemed to be catering only for the fabulously wealthy.

Now, I am guessing here, but I am presuming that the YHA was badly hit when the Covid lockdown put the kibosh on many people's travels during 2020 and, as a reaction, it has relooked at its business model, coming up with this alterative solution. But is it really generating more money? Looking at the availability calendar for Pwll Deri, there are only a handful of dates throughout the year when the hostel appears to have been booked for Exclusive Hire; most of the time, it is just standing empty; unavailable for walkers like me who would love to be able to make use of one of their empty beds; not bringing in a *sou* in terms of revenue for the YHA.

And it is not just Pwll Deri that is only available for Exclusive Hire. The YHA website states that it has "100 unique properties in top locations across England and Wales, perfectly placed to explore hidden gems and national treasures." Just not for lone travellers, like me.

In the end, the unavailability of any accommodation in Pwll Deri forced me to rethink my entire trip to Pembrokeshire, with the corresponding knock on effect of a loss of revenue for the nice-looking B&B overlooking the beach at Broad Haven; the fancy inn at Porthgain; and the glamping pod, I'd got my eye on, south of Solva.

In the past, the YHA has always been a byword for healthy, youthful, outdoorsy exploration and endeavour; it is like the Duke of Edinburgh's Award in bricks and mortar; Enid Blyton's Famous Five all crammed into one bunk bed. I hope that long and admirable tradition is not going to change such that all the YHA becomes synonymous with is exclusive stag and hen parties.

10 Top Takeaways from Walking the Ridgeway

I walked The Ridgeway national trail from Avebury to Ivinghoe Beacon over eight days in September 2023. These are my top ten takeaways from the experience.

1. Compeed plasters are second to none.
2. Chalk paths are very slippery when wet.
3. Don't judge a walk by its start (or finish). The official start/end of The Ridgeway is Overton Hill, which is nothing more than an uninspiring carpark, and which looks more suitable for doggers than walkers. The end/start of The Ridgeway is Ivinghoe Beacon, which has glorious views but, at the precise moment that I completed my walk, was being hogged by two of the most unaware, loud-mouthed, arrogant cyclists I have ever had the misfortune to encounter.
4. If you have zips on your rucksack, make sure they are zipped up together at the **side**, not at the **top** of the bag. I discovered this simple lesson when I found my rucksack gaping open whilst walking through the Aston Rowant Nature Reserve and had to retrace my steps a mile in order to recover a jacket, which had fallen out.
5. Toilet paper makes a good page divider when your guidebook has got soaking wet. Another lesson learned through bitter experience when a month's rain fell on Smeathe's Ridge in one hour.
6. Book accommodation as close to the trail as is possible. Although the official trail length is 87 miles, I estimated that I walked a further 26 miles getting to my overnight stops.
7. Cheese sandwiches and a Mars bar make a perfectly nutritious lunch every day for a week.

8. Flints can feel very hard underfoot even when wearing the sturdiest walking boots.
9. Waterproof doesn't mean storm-proof. See 5.
10. Despite depressing (and accurate) warnings concerning the loss of Britain's biodiversity, England remains a very green and pleasant land.

A High Point in Rye

It was the kind of situation where if I had been discovered dead, impaled by the church weather vane no one would have shown me any sympathy; instead, would have said: "What was she thinking being up there in the first place."

It had not been my intention to climb to the top of the tower of St Mary's Church, Rye when I had woken up that day; in fact, it had not been my intention to climb to the top of the tower of St Mary's Church, Rye a mere ten minutes before I accomplished the feat but, like so many similar summit assaults what can you do when you discover 'it is there'?

The payment of £4 to an elderly(ish) woman sat a desk just inside the church foyer permitted me to enter a door to her left, and start climbing a narrow staircase, which in turn gave way to an even narrower corridor, which ended at a second, even narrower, staircase.

The staircase decanted at a rather large, square room, wood-panelled and red-carpeted, the walls of which were adorned with all kinds of (doubtlessly) worthy and interesting information about the church and its tower, but I was in no mood to stop and peruse; the summit fever was upon me; onwards and upwards.

Would you call it a ladder? I'll be generous and say a wooden staircase headed heavenwards. The rungs—do you have rungs on a staircase?—were steep. I continued undaunted. A second ladder—this one was definitely more a ladder than a staircase—led to the bell tower. I vaguely remembered that there had been a notice at the start of the ascent warning that the bells sounded every hour. I glanced at my watch. Quarter past. I had plenty of leeway before a potential deafening.

Now it really was a ladder; no other word for it. I was in a realm of wooden gangways above the bells, and still heading higher. Various health and safety considerations passed through my head, but I dismissed them as being so much fuss and wussery.

Would you call it a hatchway? I'll be generous and say a door offered an invitation to the final summit of the tower. *Al fresco*, on top of the tower of St Mary's Church, Rye it was blowing a gale. It had been one of the reasons why I had entered the church in the first place; to escape the wind and rain. The parapet around the tower was quite narrow—is this becoming something of a recurring theme? At points, I had to lean backwards to avoid obstructions as I performed a wind-swept circumnavigation. Above me, the weather vane rattled and railed an angry protest against the buffeting winds. The 360° views over Rye and the surrounding countryside of Romney Marsh were a rain-obscured delight, but the stormy conditions constantly reminded me of the perilous nature of my position.

A moment's crime-fiction paranoia that the hatchway would be locked, trapping me on the tower, and I was back on the dry walkway above the bells, faced with the even more difficult task of descending the obstacle course of wooden rungs to the ground level once more, where an innocent-faced, elderly(ish) woman would still be sitting at the same desk, beside the same doorway; an unlikely Charon in church chiffon.

A Circular Walk Around Padley Gorge

Always love a circular walk. There is nothing worse than having to retrace your steps and follow the same route back. In theory, a gorge seems a pretty unpromising topographical feature for a circular walk. After all, by its very nature, it is pretty much straight and pointy, the epitome of 'there and back'. Unlike, say, the perimeter of a small island, a gorge remains defiantly linear. Nevertheless, in the case of Padley Gorge in the Peak District, it is possible to square the circle, by walking on one side of the gorge on the way out, and the other side of the gorge on the way back.

My starting point is the train station at Grindleford. Another plus-point this, a train that will take me to the very start – and end – point of my walk. The train emerging from the 3.5 mile-long Totley Tunnel, I suddenly find myself transported from Sheffield-suburbs to deep inside Peak District walking territory.

It is raining – when has it not been this year? – but I am undaunted. The route finds a degree of shelter under trees, which line the path.

This is a route walking *above* the gorge, rather than *along* the gorge and, as such, involves a certain amount of uphilling and, inevitably, downhilling. No matter how much I might study a map – and, in my case, this is never for very long – I always find myself caught out by the contour lines. The actual land is always more hilly than the – flat – map would give me to believe. I wonder if, in another life, I had been a flat-earther.

Up, up, up, always keeping the fall-away slope of the gorge to my right-hand side. It is autumn – late autumn – and the colours of the gorge are predominately golden; the hue of leaf, either ready to fall, or already fallen forming a Yellow-Brick-Road litter on the ground. Below, the Burbage Brook, burbles noisily, following a rocky course, occasionally breaking into distinct waterfalls, always finding a route where I am less deft to follow.

Amongst the trees to my left, a short path leads to a small, ruined brick bunker, once part of Bolehill Quarry, and further on, a tree sculpture, distorted and truncated, looks like the hide of some ancient reptile.

Underfoot, it is muddy and rocky, and I help to his feet an elderly walker who has slipped whilst taking a photograph. I make sure that he is okay and carry on, my pace faster than his pace, wondering whether I should have stayed, whilst the impatience to keep to my itinerary is already driving me on.

It is nearing my turning point. The wooded path, which skirts the gorge, ends abruptly, and I emerge onto a wide plateau with a view across grassy fields to Owler Tor. A small, wooden bridge seems an unassuming crossing point from where to begin my return journey.

I make a slight refreshment detour to the National Trust property at Longshaw, where there is a café, which serves hearty bowls of soup, and it is upon leaving here that I make my mistake; think that I can be clever; decide I can cut off a corner by taking an unmarked path by the side of the pond.

I find myself in a walled paddock. Sheep stare at me like the stranger than I am. Is that a gate on the far side? It isn't, but it takes me the time to walk across the paddock to discover this. I retrace my steps. The very thing that I had been hoping to avoid on a circular walk, I am obliged to do, because I have ventured off piste. I am momentarily distracted watching a small roe deer, but she appears to be just as lost as me.

I am conscious that the afternoon is drawing on, and it will begin to get dark shortly. The rocky paths of the gorge are no place to be walking in the twilight, let alone in darkness. I hurry on, reassured that I have the steep sides of the gorge beside me again. It is not long before I have a distant view of a road still far below, and close to it what appears to be Grindleford Station.

The track heads steeply down; more treacherous than the going-up. I wonder how far this path will take me, when, as if by magic, I find myself on a short track directly beside the station café.

The rain is still falling, but I only have ten minutes to wait for a train to take me back to Sheffield, and it is not yet dark outside by the time that the Totley Tunnel engulfs me once more.

A Good Sport at the Sportsman

It is always good to have a definite objective in mind at the start of a long walk and, on a recent 12-mile circular walk from Faversham that objective was The Sportsman pub at Seasalter. I hadn't been to The Sportsman for years; decades. Little did I know it, but that absence was going to prove my undoing.

I set out from Faversham early on a wet summer morning. I planned to walk to Seasalter by the countryside route via Goodnestone, arriving at the pub in good time for lunch and a well-deserved pint, and then returning via the footpath, which hugs the estuary and Faversham Creek.

It did not take long to leave the town of Faversham behind and hit open fields. Anticipating a steady drizzle to be my own companion, it came as something of a surprise to encounter a veritable crowd in the ploughed field ahead. Detectorists, undeterred by the damp conditions. There were more than thirty of them. For some reason, I found their silent sweepings slightly sinister that wet morning—rather more AntiquiSearchers than DMDC. I recalled the advice of Andy and Lance from *Detectorists* and, as a rambler in their territory, I refrained from asking if they had found any gold; in fact, I gave them a wide berth altogether, whilst still surreptitiously surveying the ploughed earth beneath my walking boots for the merest glint of Anglo Saxon treasure.

I crossed the railway line—always an event, which provokes a slight thrill—to be propelled into a world of vast polytunnels and intensive farming. The crop was strawberries; and a farm, which yields over 10 tonnes of the fruit each day. I could have picked a couple of pounds myself but I resist, mindful of building up an appetite for the lunch at The Sportsman ahead.

I look into the fine Norman churches at both Goodnestone and Graveney, without taking in anything about their histories and, in a brief moment of sunshine, cross fields of golden barley, flecked with red poppies. But, by the time that the short line of beach huts at Seasalter has become the dominant feature on the horizon, the rain has started to fall again in earnest and I am feeling hungry and rather dispirited. The Sportsman appears as a welcome sanctuary to a tired walker.

However, a notice on the door of the pub gives warning of a possible problem: FULLY BOOKED. Fully booked? This is not The Sportsman that I remember with its door always open to any passing itinerant. Times change. My muddy, bedraggled figure is greeted at the door with a critically appraising look and a:

“Do you have a reservation?”

“No,” I am obliged to confess, as the rain continues to fall on me.

“I’m very sorry, but we are fully booked for today’s five-course taster-menu.”

Five-course taster-menu? Visions of a sustaining pork pie are quickly vanishing.

While I continue to stand in the cold, the occupants of a large BMW are hastily ushered past me into the warmth and shelter beyond; there is little need to ask if they have a reservation.

"Can I just get a drink?" I persist.

In the end, I think that it must have been my rain-soaked forlorn appearance, which swung it; that or a vestigial throwback to the hospitality of The Sportsman of old, which was renowned as a walker's pub. A chair was brought out to me in the conservatory; a pint of Whitstable Bay beer put in front of me. I felt rather like the dog being served a bowl of water, but I was grateful for the courtesy extended.

From inside the pub, enticing snippets of conversation, richly voiced, like a bevy of Rowley Birkins, reached my ears: "Blah, blah… particularly fine sausages… blah, blah."

I felt a sense of disappointment about the change, which had overtaken a pub that I had known of old, but it was a change that was perhaps inevitable. Adapt or go under. The simple fact was that I had been a solitary walker on my footpath that day; my custom alone would not have sustained a viable business model. In comparison, the BMWs and Mercedes were myriad; the five-course taster-menu was clearly popular, just to a different clientele from the walkers of old. I wondered if I would ever be back again? Probably not, unless I was driven there in an expensive car.

Finishing my drink, I ventured into the pub's toilets, where I was amused to encounter an embarrassed five-courser sticking out her bum to dry the seat of her designer white jeans at the hot air dryer.

Even the five-coursers were not completely immune from the weather.

The rain had subsided by the time that I returned to my route, following the easily-navigable coastal path of the Saxon Shore Way. I nibbled a bag of crisps—not the pork pie that I had dreamed about, but good-enough for a hungry rambler. I paused briefly to photograph a curlew—there had been an item on the local news only that morning saying that their numbers were falling. I hoped to spot an avocet, but no such luck.

Storm clouds threatened on the horizon, but for the time being they passed me by. An old brown-sailed barge kept me company, plying a route in the same direction, through the mudflats and wind farms of the estuary. Opposite from the sea, longhorn cattle and marsh sheep—the rams rather sinister-looking with their three horns—had their heads down, feasting rather more abundantly than had I.

Turning at Faversham Creek, I was suddenly conscious that the tall, distinctive spire of St Mary of Charity Church in Faversham still appeared a long way distant across the flats and creeks—a helluva long way distant—and I picked up my pace, keen to get back to the town by mid-afternoon. However, as is often the case, distances proved deceptive, and it was not long before the familiar sight of the Oyster Bay House on Standard Quay was ahead of me, signalling the end of my walk and, just around the corner, the even more welcome sight of The Anchor and, what might just be, the most welcome plate of fish and chips in the world.

The Abandoned Barges of Maple Cross

It is just a skeleton of a building. The old Harefield Limeworks on the bank of the Grand Union Canal. It is the haunt of urban explorers; sometimes described as one of the creepiest sites in London; popularly known as the Hanging Monkey Building, because of the vast, stuffed primate, which inexplicably hangs from a hoist, high up, overlooking the canal. Google cites the Limeworks as 'temporarily closed'. It would take something more than an optimist to imagine that this building will ever return to being a going concern in the foreseeable future.

The Harefield Limeworks is not the only sign of an old industrial past along this stretch of the Grand Union Canal, close to Maple Cross, between Rickmansworth and Denham. It can be witnessed in a painting of a horse towing a barge, running the full length of a wall of one of the longest tunnels on this stretch of the waterway; also in the numerous old transport barges, which line the canal bank, many rusting from disuse; several waterlogged and filled with rubbish, gradually disappearing under the surface of the canal's waters.

There is something more picturesque about these ruined barges than their work-a-day neighbours; the idea of the 'ruin' a familiar romantic trope of European art, literature and aesthetics since the 18th century. Then, artists and poets admired the crumbling castles and churches of a previous age; today, graffiti artists and Instagrammers choose for their backdrops the harsh metal and concrete wastelands of our industrial heritage.

However, this stretch of the canal is not all about industry. Nature is never far away. Indeed, adjacent to the Maple Lodge Sewage Treatment Works—"Is it just me, or can you smell that?—is the largest area of reedbeds in London: Springwell Reedbed. This is a home of warblers and, at the time I visited, a family of baby coots, their bright red furry heads in marked contrast to their sleek black parents. There are swans and mallards on the canal; several cormorants in the high branches of the trees; and a red kite ever-watchful, circling overhead. Colourful butterflies flit across the towpath, and white cherry blossom and fluffy catkins grow along the bank of the canal.

I don't dally too long; I have my own rendezvous ahead with some culinary and cultural heritage: a pint of cider and a sausage roll. At a point where the Grand Union Canal, the River Colne and Pynesfield

Lake run so close together that dry land is at a premium stands the welcomingly solid edifice of the Coy Carp Inn. I cross a bridge to enter, taking my victuals to an outside table overlooking the water, where another coot sits on a nest of reeds, tutting at me irritably. In a field opposite, a rider ties up her horse, both equally wide of beam; and, overhead, the sun penetrates around the edge of my table's umbrella. The abandoned barges might belong to a near-forgotten past, but it suddenly feels as though an English summer is not far away.

The Beauty of the Tulip Stairs

What is it about stairs? Of all practical architectural features, they seem to have the greatest capacity for beauty. Previously, I have admired George Gilbert Scott's fine staircase in the Renaissance Hotel at St Pancras, and the magnificent spiral sweep of the Scala Contarini del Bovolo in Venice. In order to visit the Tulip Stairs, my treads take me to Greenwich and the Queen's House.

The Tulip Stairs are the work of the acclaimed English architect Inigo Jones, and were completed in 1635 during the reign of Charles I. They were the first self-supporting spiral staircase in Britain, with cantilevers in the wall supporting the structure, leaving an Instagrammable unimpeded view up through the centre of the staircase. The white stairs are lined by a fine, wrought-iron balustrade of blue-painted flowers.

The purity of the spiral, combined with the simplicity of the colours produces a thing of beauty, best viewed from the ground floor where the soaring spiral ascends towards a summit into pure abstraction.

At the time of my visit, a school party of teenagers crowded the hallowed stairs; hung over the beautiful bannisters; somewhat spoiled the awesome aesthetic. No need for anxiety, though: bored youth does not linger long, and I soon have the staircase to myself, except for the earnest tripod-wielding, slowly-shutter-adjusting camera-buff, who I recognise will not be so easily dislodged as the chattering youthful masses. Grudgingly, I accept his proximity; prepare to share my moment of the sublime; recognise that this is the reality of the big city and mass tourism; acknowledge that my presence is as annoying to him as his is to me.

The Excitement of Incomprehension

I count myself fortunate to have been able to travel to many different countries in the world but, for all the countries I have visited, I remain singularly inept at speaking any languages other than English.

Now, I know that this is a common English cliché. English people have a reputation for being notoriously sluggish about learning different languages; an unwillingness helped by the fact that so many people overseas are very proficient at speaking English. However, I am not so sure that I fall into this particular stereotype.

I actively enjoy the fact that when I travel abroad I can understand very little. Far from being a hindrance, I find my lack of comprehension a positive asset. It adds to the excitement of being in a new place; increases the sensation of 'otherness'. I also find my lack of understanding surprisingly restful. Whereas in an English-speaking country, I am continually bombarded by unwanted information: programmes on the TV; signs in shop windows; people's overheard conversations; headlines on newspapers; advertisements and posters; when I am overseas, all of this uninvited stimuli diminishes to a pleasant background blur. Written language becomes nothing more than pretty pictures; spoken language simply random sounds. To immerse myself in this world of incomprehension is like taking a detox from the 21st century.

I find the same principle also works when it comes to religion. There is little I enjoy more than listening to a Latin mass in a tiny church far removed from anywhere that I consider familiar to me. I invariably achieve a sense of personal spirituality by allowing myself to be swept along listening to the solemn cadence, immune to the meaning of the bewildering jumble of unknown words. It is only with understanding that I find my spiritual bubble bursts. For me, neither William Tyndale nor King James did me any favours. I like both my religion and my overseas travels served up in unfathomably unintelligible doses.

A Message to Manufacturers of Wheelie-Bags

Predictable as night follows day is the fact that the wheels on my wheelie bag will let me down. Again.

I have lost count of the number of perfectly good suitcases I have had to chuck away, simply because the wheels have become so worn down that they no longer function. They are a persistent point of weakness on an otherwise solid construction.

My latest wheelie bag had come with a five-year guarantee, which still had two years to run, so I returned the case to the retailer from whom I had originally bought it. They eyed the case a bit suspiciously and said that they would need to consult the manufacturer. Fine, I thought. I had long been campaigning for a change of design to wheelie bag wheels; have them replaceable, rather than sealed units, which cannot be readily removed. Here, I hoped, might be a manufacturer prepared to make a change; would look at my case, recognise the fault in their design, and come up with an entirely new construction for wheelie bag wheels.

Not so. The report came back from the manufacturer to the retailer regarding my case with a rather blunt statement that they did not believe that the damage to the wheels could have resulted from 'normal use' and that they would not honour the guarantee. Thankfully, the retailer took a different viewpoint and did honour the guarantee, but it left a bad taste.

What is considered 'normal use'?

The bag had let me down on a recent two-week *rundfahrt* in Germany. I had trailed it between train station and accommodation in several cities, including a mile or so across old East German pavements in Berlin; a couple of miles on smooth streets in Dresden; and a mile along a rough, gravel track in Oberammergau but, there, I had taken pity on the bag and actually carried it for half the journey. This is my 'normal use'.

If a bag comes with a five-year guarantee, I expect that I should be able to wheel it with me for every mile I walk during those five years and it will still keep rolling. I don't live my entire life on soft carpets, and I don't expect my wheelie bag to require any more pampering than I do.

I looked online to see if other people had trouble with the wheels on their wheelie bags. And, judging by the number of instructional videos on Youtube, showing how it is possible to replace worn-down wheels—not easily, in most cases—I get the impression that my problem is pretty universal.

In a time when we should be limiting the amount of waste we produce, I am forced to chuck away a perfectly good suitcase simply because one small element of it is designed to fail. In the spirit of saving resources, I would urge the manufacturers of wheelie bags to relook at their products and fit them with wheels that can be removed and replaced.

In the meantime, I have been amused to see that my new wheelie bag now comes with a ten-year guarantee. Ten years! Until the manufacturers change their product, I'll be seeing you again within three.

Fitting My Own Wheelie-Bag Wheels

Another year, another pair of wheelie-bag wheels worn through; another disbelieving response when I apply for a refund against my guarantee. This time, it was on the platform of Tring railway station where my bag's wheels finally gave up the ghost; this time, the manufacturer wanted me to send the entire bag back to them 'for analysis'. Preposterous!

Bored of this annual stand-off, I decide to look for an alternative solution.

And I may have found one.

The rest of my suitcase is perfectly serviceable; as always, it is only the wheels, which prove a constant point of weakness. If I could just replace the wheels…

With some of my earlier cases, the wheel attachment had been moulded as an integral part of the case itself, and so could not be replaced. However, my current case is a different proposition. Carefully unzipping the inner fabric lining—revealing a smuggler's dream hidden compartment—I discovered that the wheels were simply screwed through the hard outer fabric of the case. If I could find replacement wheels to fit the same dimensions…

When in need, turn to Amazon. And, as always, Amazon supplied. Three days later—and still resisting Prime's next day delivery—a small parcel appeared on my doorstep, and I set to the task of repairing my broken wheelie-bag.

Phillips-head screwdriver in hand, the job of removing the useless, old wheels was relatively easy. Attaching the new ones was no much more difficult, although it required slightly more precision lining-up and much swearing.

Fifteen minutes, a slightly sore palm, and my wheelie-bag was as good as new. Better even. The new wheels looked more robust and sturdy than the old ones; more made of the right stuff.

Or were they?

Always, at the back of my mind, there will be a nagging doubt surrounding my own workmanship. Will the bag ever be as good as when it first rolled off the production line of the original manufacturers? Have I unwittingly committed some DIY faux pas, which will only manifest itself when I embark on my next travels?

Only Time will tell. My newly-repaired wheelie-bag may last for five years, or a wayward wheel may roll off on my first outing out-of-doors. Whatever, in case I ever need to make running repairs, I may make a Phillips-head screwdriver my constant travelling companion.

Around the World

On Board a UFO in Bratislava

It felt rather like being whisked away by aliens. It was something of a spur of the moment decision to go to Bratislava. I was staying in Vienna, with no intention of travelling any further east. But then I happened to glance at a train timetable, and it was only an hour's journey between the two cities, and I just thought, why the hell not.

And I was so pleased that I decided to make that journey to Slovakia.

Part of my reason for deciding to visit, was to see the Danube. Although the Danube also runs through Vienna, it is not such an integral part of the old city there as it is in Bratislava. So, when I arrived at Bratislava Hlavna Stanica train station, and without a map to guide me, I simply allowed my feet to follow a downhill course in the assumption that I would eventually arrive at the river. Which half an hour later, I did. But before I saw the river, I spotted the UFO.

Standing at 95 metres, the UFO Tower is home to an open-air observation deck and restaurant at the southern end of the Most

SNP (Most Slovenského národného povstania), the principal bridge spanning the Danube in the centre of Bratislava. The observation deck is shaped like the classic Sci-Fi interpretation of a flying saucer, and is accessed by a lift in the east leg of the structure. It seemed like the perfect vantage point to get the view of the Danube, which I was craving.

The lift was small and fast and, judging from the construction of the tower, must have risen in a course slightly off-vertical, but I was not aware of this anomaly when inside. Within 45 seconds, I was at the level of the panoramic restaurant, from which a short staircase led up to the observation deck.

From such a high position, it was possible to truly appreciate the scale and majesty of the Danube. It is a vast river. Powerful, too. The current was strong; a wide array of flotsam, including entire tree trunks, was being propelled downstream, whilst pleasure boats and sleek Leviathan-like river-cruise ships were making slow headway upstream.

To the north lay the red roofs of the old town, with Bratislava Castle prominent on a tree-fringed mount. To the south, modern wide carriageways led into a world of apartment blocks and industrial parks.

I lingered long, watching the city from my surreal space-ship; the open expanse of river magnifying the sounds of the streets, making me feel simultaneously connected to, and disconnected from, the earthlings below. It was a fresh breeze and the slightest hint of drizzle, which finally drove me back indoors. I might have been persuaded to halt for a while to grab something to eat in the restaurant, but I didn't think there would be a seat that would match the view I had experienced on the observation deck. Although in that belief, I was soon to be proved wrong.

One last call before I took the lift back to ground level: the toilet. Here, the view from the Ladies, would take a lot of beating.

Finding Beauty in Brasília

The recent (January 2023) riot by supporters of Jair Bolsonaro, in which government buildings in Brasília were stormed by an angry mob, threw an unwelcome spotlight on a capital city, which is often overshadowed by the more populous São Paulo and the more glamorous Rio de Janeiro. For me, though, I have fonder memories of Brasília than either of its noisy neighbours.

Designed as a purpose-built capital city by architect Oscar Niemeyer and urban planner Lúcio Costa, I visited thirty years after its inauguration. At the time, I was struck by the wide open spaces of the capital; its modernist buildings; its beautiful churches.

As a tourist, it felt somewhere that was safe to wander around; local people spoke of how there was no need to lock up their houses; the atmosphere was far more relaxed than the big cities on the coast. There was talk of an urban utopia.

Thirty years later, and the talk is more of an urban dystopia. Brasília's initial success has ultimately led to its downfall. Over-crowding has resulted in a gridlocked traffic system and the zonal demarcation of services has led to sprawling residential districts without access to local amenities. Art critic Robert Hughes was very critical of the city as long ago as 1980 in his landmark TV documentary series *The Shock of the New*.

And yet, for all its problems, I can't help but find that the modernist beauty of its centre remains. It may not work for its residents but, for a visitor, I still felt as though I had arrived at a city located on a different planet. It was rather like walking through a slightly dodgy stage set for a futurist city on *Doctor Who*. And I felt thrilled. Any moment, I expected ten-foot tall humanoid aliens dressed in tightly-fitting Spandex body stockings to walk up and approach me and welcome me to their world.

Hughes stated of Brasília that 'nothing dates faster than people's fantasies about the future' but, the fact is, that I still prefer my science fiction to be of 1950s vintage rather than anything that has come out more recently. Why bother with Banks when you can have a bit of Dick has long been a design-for-living that I adhere to.

So, for me, I retain happy memories, strolling on that hot, high plateau in the centre of Brazil, amidst a deserted, concrete world of grand government structures, long empty vistas, and the hopes of a better world.

Fond Memories of the Southerner

It was only recently, when friends talked about planning a holiday travelling on New Zealand's train network – although I am not sure that network is quite the right term for the few lines that still exist – that I discovered that the *Southerner* has been discontinued. Admittedly, I was rather slow to catch up on this news. Twenty-one years to be precise. The Southerner has not run since 2002.

I was fortunate enough to travel on the *Southerner* in 1992. God, what a train. I picked up the *Southerner* in Kaikoura, on the east coast of New Zealand's South Island, venturing south as far as Dunedin – a city, which to my shame, I pronounced at the time as Dun-EEE-din. Looking back now, with the benefit of hindsight, I wish that I had taken the *Southerner* all the way to Invercargill; at the time the most southerly destination, which could be reached by train.

My memory of the *Southerner* was that it was surprisingly slow – the best part of 6 hours just to travel the 200-mile leg between Christchurch and Dunedin - particularly for what was designated as an 'express' train, but also that I was perfectly happy for it to dawdle along as slowly as it liked. I didn't care how long it took to arrive; I could have quite happily lived on the *Southerner*.

It was August – NZ winter – and it was blimin' cold outside. Inside the *Southerner*, it was warm. And it was comfortable. My memory is of wide seats, covered with sheepskin. Could this have been possible? I would happily believe wood panels lined the walls, but this would have been a false memory. Whatever, it was luxurious. I had been bed-hopping from one cold, cheap hostel dormitory to hostel dormitory; whilst, here, was genuine comfort. Travellers' accounts seem most often to reminisce about the *Southerner's* dining car; I never made use of this facility, but I still found the experience of travelling on the *Southerner* a delight.

Outside the *Southerner* was a dark, harsh, cold environment but, within its reassuring embrace, all was calm; all was safe.

Dunedin Station – respect due; it's a magnificent building – was finally reached with a modicum of regret. I knew a new adventure lay ahead of me – mainly involving Yellow-eyed Penguins, Royal Albatrosses and New Zealand fur seals at Taiaroa Head on the Otago Peninsula – but I could already picture the backpacker hostel, which would be my temporary home: shared rooms; cold beds; having to raid the house-keeper's store-cupboard for extra blankets.

The *Southerner's* sheepskin seats were already fading to a distant memory.

Crimean Tatars and Gold Medals in Red Square

I always imagined that one day I would travel on the Trans-Siberian Railway from Moscow to Vladivostok. Now I am not so sure.

So, I am grateful for having visited Russia (USSR at the time) back in July 1987. It was a rare window of opportunity, during the period of Glasnost when Mikhail Gorbachev was leader of the Soviet Union.

To give it some historical and cultural context, my visit occurred two months after German aviator Mathias Rust famously landed his small civilian Cessna aircraft on Bolshoy Moskvoretsky Bridge close to Red Square; over two years before David Hasselhoff sang on top of the Berlin Wall; and four years before the dissolution of the Soviet Union in 1991.

God, I was young back then. Young with rather hazy memories, and a set of blurry photographs.

The extent of my visit to the vast expanses of the Union of Soviet Socialist Republics was limited to Moscow. I stayed in the Rossiya Hotel, adjacent to Red Square and one of the largest hotels in the world. It was a typical Soviet-era hotel. Big and blocky; authoritarian-bleak in a time before authoritarian-chic; with a stereotypically stern-faced, wide-beamed *dezhurnaya*, sitting behind a desk, guarding both the keys and the morals of the hotel floor.

I could see the colourful domes of St Basil's Cathedral from the hotel; at the time, it was the one iconic image of Moscow that I could readily identify. On my first evening in the city, I was drawn towards this familiar landmark, attempting to find reassurance in something that was known and recognisable. However, I found my way blocked. Every entrance to Red Square was sealed off; uniformed militiamen held back a growing crowd of bemused onlookers. It was clear that few people knew what was going on. Unable to speak or understand Russian, I could not make out what the local Muscovites were saying, but most seemed as confused as the small gaggle of tourists. Suddenly, I found that I was not alone. A short, middle-aged man had singled me out from amongst the crowd of strangers. He was clearly Russian but spoke good English:

"It is the Crimean Tatars," he explained. "They are demanding the right to return to their homelands, which were taken from them under Stalin. They are staging a vigil in the middle of Red Square. One of them is threatening to set himself on fire."

With the selfish single-mindedness of youth, I was not so much interested in the concerns of the Tatars as I was the more practical question of when Red Square would be accessible again. The man shrugged. Here was a question that no one could answer.

We continued to watch the Square companionably for several more minutes and then, as I was preparing to leave, the short man pressed something into my hand.

"Here, for you."

It had been a rather surreptitious manoeuvre, and I opened my palm, suspicious of what I would see. Something hard and shiny. And heavy. A coin? No. I looked more closely at what appeared to be an Olympic gold medal. It was baffling, and rather frightening. Upon initially entering the USSR, there had been strict customs checks and declarations about the amount of foreign currency that it was permissible to bring in—and out; I had little doubt that an Olympic gold medal would not be something that could be easily explained away upon my exit simply as 'a gift'. I thanked the man and handed back his present. I explained the problem about taking items across the border. He looked slightly hurt, but we parted as friends, leaving me with a lot of unanswered questions. It had been an interesting first evening in Moscow.

Remembering VDNKh

It was a hot day that trip to the USSR Exhibition of Achievements of the National Economy (*Vystavka dostizheniy narodnovo khozyaystva* - VDKNh). The park lies about ten kilometres north of Red Square, Moscow and covers a vast area, the size of a small town. I visited in 1987 as part of an Intourist tour.

I remember that I was suffering from something of a hangover. The evening before, there had been a banquet—also laid on by Intourist––with multiple courses, and where between every course a—generous—shot of vodka was raised and drunk as a toast. At the time, I was quite a fan of vodka, and drunk my shots with alacrity, but they had left me less-than-enthusiastic for the next day's outing. Just outside the exhibition park, I discovered a vending machine, which appeared to despatch fresh apple juice, which I thought might provide something of a cure for my aching head. Unfortunately, the hot weather must have done something detrimental to the ingredients. The apple juice had fermented producing a toxic brew, far more potent even than the spirits that I had partaken the evening before. It was with something like horror that I watched mothers queueing up at the machine, unsuspectingly handing the intoxicating brew to their young children as a refreshing thirst-quencher. If I had had the language, I might have warned them; instead, I could only stand and stare.

The entrance to the exhibition area was an archway of Triomphe proportions. The Parisian theme was continued, with a series of ornate fountains, which would not have been out of place at Versailles. However, the Socialist Classicism-style skyscrapers, which loomed over the background recalled that this was a brainchild of Stalin and not of a Louis.

In my rather foggy-headed state, I visited one exhibit after another, perhaps inevitably most impressed by the pavilion dedicated to the Soviet space programme, complete with an enormous Vostok rocket. Equally impressive was the enormous statue featuring a man and a woman holding a hammer and sickle dedicated to the workers in a Socialist Realism-style—Worker and Kolkhoz Woman (*Rabóchiy i kolkhóznitsa*).

My Intourist guide solemnly explained display after display with a dutiful but resigned sense of patriotism, but it was obvious that his real enthusiasm was reserved for the Beryozka shop, where he explained that he was not allowed to buy anything because they only accepted foreign currency, but where he had a long shopping list pre-prepared in the hope that some of his overseas charges would make the various purchases he wanted on his behalf.

Raffles, Singapore

Turning out the contents of an old box in the attic, I came across some travel ephemera, which transported me several decades back in time and several thousand miles' distance in space.

It was a place mat and a fading receipt from Raffles Hotel in Singapore; the Long Bar at Raffles Hotel, to be more precise.

Raffles Hotel has long stood as an icon of colonialism, and the height of decadency has always been to enjoy a Singapore Gin Sling in the shady comfort of the hotel's Long Bar, following in the footsteps of such notable guests as Charlie Chaplin, Elizabeth Taylor, Somerset Maugham and Rudyard Kipling. I was fortunate enough to visit the Long Bar in its original setting in the hotel's lobby, before a major makeover of the hotel relocated it to a neighbouring shopping arcade.

Legend has it that the cocktail was the invention of Raffles' barman Ngiam Tong Boon in 1915, and is a concoction of Beefeater Gin, Bénédictine, pineapple juice, lime juice, Angostura bitters, and Peter Heering cherry liqueur, giving it a delicate reddish hue.

I settled into one of the Long Bar's large, rattan bucket-chairs, feeling slightly conspicuously alone at my table with my tall, eye-catching drink. Not that I needed to worry: it was late morning, before the lunchtime rush, and I had the place almost to myself. Outside the temperature was in the 90s, with the humidity even higher but, inside, the atmosphere was as cool as the ice in my cocktail.

At the time, my gin sling cost nine Singapore dollars, which was a fairly considerable sum; nowadays, I understand that the price is four times that amount. Notoriety does not come cheap. However, I was able to while away a very pleasant, relaxing hour, undisturbed and unruffled; and, it was well worth it, simply to discover a serene, fan-chilled time-capsule, protected from the oppressive bustle and clamminess of the modern world happening outside.

The drink must have been pretty intoxicating, too, because when I left I seem to acquire a Raffles Hotel towel, of which I have very little memory.

The Most Walkable Cities in the World (if You Don't Like Walking)

Recent research by Preply has ascertained a list of the most walkable cities in Europe, based on the distance required to walk between that city's five most-highly rated tourist attractions. Top of the list comes Seville, which has only a mile, or 2,100 steps, between Seville Cathedral, the Real Alcázar, Plaza de España, La Giralda, and the Barrio Santa Cruz district. Cities making up the rest of the Top Five include Venice, Porto, Florence, and Athens. At the other end of the scale, the least walkable cities include Lisbon, Zagreb, and Hamburg.

I find the research interesting, but I have a few issues.

Firstly… Venice? The second most walkable city? Okay, if measured in pure distance but, as anyone who has ever visited Venice will know, your walk will be at a snail's pace, following the same few streets behind a horde of similarly slow-moving fellow-travellers.

Also, the parameters as specified by the research means that the data can be easily skewed by a single outlier. Just one top-rated attraction lying outside the bounds of the city centre would be enough to adversely affect that city's rank on the list.

However, I have a much bigger beef with the survey than these minor quibbles. Preply's idea of *most* walkable is somewhere that means you walk the *least* distance. Is that a definition of *most* walkable, or *least* walkable? Personally, I like walking. I don't want the shortest walk; I am looking for the most interesting walk. I don't want to have a gentle amble for a measly mile; I want to be out tramping for an entire day until the leather of my shoes is hot and my feet are tired.

Next stop Lisbon then.

Printed in Great Britain
by Amazon

57069346R00059